D0385875

THE REBBETZIN

A BRIEF BIOGRAPHY

THE REBBETZIN
CHAYA MUSHKA SCHNEERSON
A BRIEF BIOGRAPHY

Published and Copyrighted © 1999
Third Printing—January 2021
by
KEHOT PUBLICATION SOCIETY
770 Eastern Parkway / Brooklyn, New York 11213
(718) 774-4000 / Fax (718) 774-2718
editor@kehot.com / www.kehot.org

ORDERS:
291 Kingston Avenue / Brooklyn, New York 11213
(718) 778-0226 / Fax (718) 778-4148
www.kehot.com

3 5 7 9 11 12 10 8 6 4

LC Record available at: https://lccn.loc.gov/2005357549

ISBN 978-0-8266-0101-8

Printed in China

PREFACE
to first printing

We are proud to present the first in a series of brief biographies of the Chabad-Lubavitch dynasty.

This year marks the eleventh anniversary of the passing of Rebbetzin Chaya Mushka, wife of the Lubavitcher Rebbe, Rabbi Menachem M. Schneerson, of blessed memory and daughter of the sixth Lubavitcher Rebbe, Rabbi Yosef Yitzchak Schneersohn, of blessed memory. We begin the series with her biography.

MERKOS L'INYONEI CHINUCH
Brooklyn, New York
Shevat 22, 5759 (1999)

FAMILY TREE

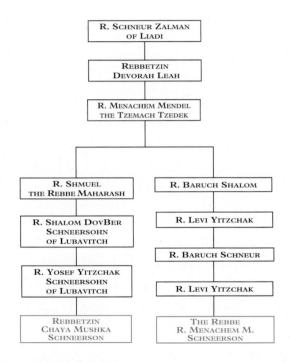

This chart traces the lineage of the Rebbetzin and her husband, the Rebbe, to Rabbi Schneur Zalman of Liadi, founder of Chabad-Lubavitch.

BIRTH

*R*ebbetzin Chaya (Moussia) Mushka Schneerson was born in Babinovitch, near the Russian city of Lubavitch, on Shabbat, the 25th of Adar, in 1901. She was the second of three daughters of the sixth Lubavitcher Rebbe, Rabbi Yosef Yitzchak and his wife, Rebbetzin Nechama Dina Schneersohn.

When she was born, her grandfather, the fifth Lubavitcher Rebbe, Rabbi Shalom DovBer who was abroad, telegraphed her father the follow- ing, "...*Mazal tov on the birth of your daugh- ter... if she has not yet been named, she should be called Chaya Mushka (the name of the wife of the T'zemach T'zedek)."*

Rabbi Shalom DovBer

From her earliest years, the Rebbetzin absorbed the purity and holiness that surrounded her, both in the house of her grandfather and that of her father.

EARLY YEARS

During World War I, in the autumn of 1915, Chaya Mushka and her family fled Lubavitch and settled in Rostov. While in Rostov, Rabbi Shalom DovBer became ill, and nineteen-year-old Chaya Mushka affectionately cared for her grandfather, spending nights at his side. Before his passing in 1920, Rabbi Shalom DovBer blessed Chaya Mushka and left several Chasidic classics to her in his last will.

Her early twenties saw the intensification

of the Communist war against the Jewish soul and the beginning of her father's heroic struggle. During those dark Soviet nights, Rabbi Yosef Yitzchak had his daughter Chaya Mushka at his side.

Rabbi Yosef Yitzchak

Cognizant of her wisdom and strength, her father involved her in much of his work. Young Chaya Mushka was asked to secretly transport food and supplies to Rostov's underground Yeshiva, in the knowledge that she could be relied upon for her discerning judgment.

Rebbetzin Chaya Mushka in her youth

Life became increasingly dangerous for the Jews of Rostov, and in the spring of 1924 her family moved to Leningrad, where Chaya Mushka's involvement continued.

In a recently discovered document dated December 4, 1924, her father wrote:

> *I hereby empower citizen Chaya Moussia Yosepuvna (daughter of Yosef) Schneersohn, residing at Machovaya Street 12/22, apartment 10, to receive monies on my behalf or documents that are addressed to me, in all forms, from the government bank and all of its branches and offices, and from other banks, government or communal, or from other organizations or private persons or by telegraph.*

Rebbetzin Chaya Mushka was 23 years old at the time.

The persecution was relentless, and in 1927 the notorious communist police came to arrest her father in their Leningrad home. Maintaining her composure, she brilliantly managed to alert the Rebbe (her husband-

to-be) who was in the street, calling out: "Schneerson, guests have come to visit us!" Understanding her message, the Rebbe was quickly able to notify others and take the necessary precautions.

Following his arrest and imprisonment in Leningrad, her father was exiled to Kostroma, and upon his request, she was allowed to join him for the journey. On the 12th of Tammuz, she was the bearer of good news, when she notified her family in Leningrad of her father's release.

In the autumn of 1927, on the day after Simchat Torah, the Schneersohn family left the Soviet Union and moved to Riga, Latvia.

HER MARRIAGE

Before leaving Russia, Chaya Mushka was engaged to marry the Rebbe, Rabbi Menachem M. Schneerson.

For various reasons the marriage was delayed until 1928, when, on the 14th day of Kislev, their marriage was celebrated in Warsaw, Poland.

On the day preceding the wedding, thousands of Jews flocked to the railway station in Warsaw to welcome her father and his family. During the course of the day, a multitude of Chasidim, hailing from all of Poland, Lithuania, and Russia, arrived in the capital.

The Rebbetzin on her wedding day

At eight o'clock that evening, in the presence of the students of the Yeshiva Tomchei T'mimim, her father celebrated the meal of the "*chosson mohl.*" In the middle of the meal her father delivered a *maamar.* Midnight came and went, and the meal was still in progress. Her father expressed his desire to rejoice with the Yeshiva students, and they at once formed a circle, in the center of which he danced a good while.

The next day, the 14th of Kislev, at five in the evening, the *"kabbalat panim"* began. Ushers had been placed at the entrance of the Yeshiva, and only guests with official invitations were allowed to enter. Thousands of people surrounded the building and there simply wasn't enough room for them all.

Hundreds of miles away, in Russia, in Dniepropetrovsk, (Yekatrinoslav), another wedding celebration was taking place. The Rebbe's parents, Rabbi Levi Yitzchak and Rebbetzin Chana unfortunately unable to be there in person, organized a festive meal and *farbrengen* in their own house, to which they invited the local Jews.

On the 14th of Kislev—twenty five years later—the Rebbe said to his Chasidim: *"It was this day that bound me to you, and you to me..."*

Adar-I 25, 1935. Rabbi Yosef Yitzchak with his son-in-law, the Rebbe, Rabbi Menachem M. Schneerson, in Purkersdorf, Austria.

THE WAR YEARS

Following their wedding, the young couple lived in Berlin until 1933. When the Nazi regime took power in the spring of 1933, they fled to Paris.

In 1939, Germany triggered World War II by launching a *blitzkrieg* (lightning attack) against Poland. Chaya Mushka's father, aided by influential American supporters, managed to leave early in 1940 while Germany was still officially at peace with the United States. Her father miraculously arrived in the United States on the last boat to cross the Atlantic ocean before the U-boat blockade began. Once in New York City, her father set in motion efforts to rescue his family from the impending cataclysm in Europe.

In May 1940, France was invaded by German forces and surrendered within four weeks. A French puppet regime led by Marshal Philippe Petain and Pierre Laval was established in Vichy, and the Rebbe and the Rebbetzin, like most Jews, fled to Nice in southern France, choosing to live under Petain's government rather than direct Nazi occupation in Paris and the surrounding areas.

In the course of their flight, there was a devastating bombardment. As people ran in every direction, she noticed an explosive shell heading towards a man next to her. Quickly pushing him to the ground, the Rebbetzin

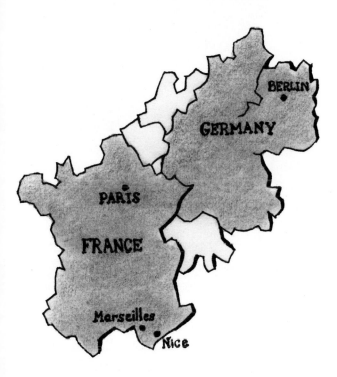

saved the man's life. Recounting this story the Rebbetzin said: *True, I saved his life, but for pushing a Jew one must do teshuvah.*

AMERICA
ESCAPING THE NAZI ONSLAUGHT

*I*n 1941, the Rebbe and the Rebbetzin boarded the Serpa Pinto and set sail (from Marseilles, France, via Lisbon, Portugal) for the United States of America.

On the 28th of Sivan, they arrived safely on the shores of America, and took up residence in New York, where her father had settled in 1940.

True, Chaya Mushka herself had escaped the Nazi claws, but she would not escape the nightmare of Europe. Her younger sister, Sheina, and her husband, Rabbi Menachem Mendel Horenstein, were still trapped in Poland when the United States declared war on Japan in December, 1941. All contact with them was lost. It was not until after the war that she and her family learned that the Horensteins had perished in the gas chambers of Treblinka.

A handwritten letter from Chaya Mushka to her father in New York, datelined Nice, 1941, informing him that visas were issued for her and the Rebbe.

"The State Department has received a telegraphic report from the Consular Officer in Marseilles...that visas were issued to Rabbi Schneerson and his wife on April 17."

17

The Rebbe, Rabbi Menachem M. Schneerson

THE REBBE'S WIFE

In 1950, upon the passing of her father, Rabbi Yosef Yitzchak Schneersohn, the leadership of the worldwide Chabad-Lubavitch movement passed to Chaya Mushka's husband. Yet, as is well known, the Rebbe initially refused to accept the position. It was his wife, the Rebbetzin, who, notwithstanding the great personal sacrifice this would entail, prevailed upon him to accept the leadership, saying: *It is simply unthinkable that father's thirty years of total self-sacrifice and accomplishment should, G-d forbid, come to naught.*

An erudite and wise woman, Rebbetzin Chaya Mushka carried the mantle of her revered and exalted position in a most humble and unpretentious fashion. All her life she fulfilled the ideal of "The entire honor of a king's daughter is within." When calling the Rebbe's office at "770," she always referred to herself simply as: "Mrs. Schneerson from President Street."

Gentle and courteous to everyone, the Rebbetzin saw her role as one wholly devoted to

The Rebbe and Rebbetzin's home, on President Street, Brooklyn

the work of her husband. Even when she relayed advice to those seeking his guidance through her, she would repeat his wording with precision, making sure that it was understood exactly as the Rebbe intended.

~

HER TRUE GREATNESS

The extraordinary respect that the Rebbe accorded to the Rebbetzin gives us a glimpse of her true stature. For although the Rebbetzin declined all public recognition, the Rebbe frequently referred to her with reverence.

Once, the Lubavitch Women's Organization sent her a bouquet of flowers, together with a list of individuals for whom blessings were requested. Setting aside the flowers for the Rebbetzin, the secretary passed on the letter to the Rebbe who, observing that it was addressed to his wife, asked his secretary to give it to her, saying: "She too is capable of giving blessings."

The Rebbe once commented to a friend of the Rebbetzin, "You have a good lawyer on your side." This was evident during a crucial time in recent Lubavitch history, during the legal proceedings to establish the ownership of the books in the Lubavitch library. When the defendant's attorney asked her: "To whom did the books belong?" the Rebbetzin answered: *My father himself, and everything he had, including the books, belong to the Chasidim.*

Her words, spoken with such sincerity made a profound impression upon the judge and helped to sway the judgment in favor of Agudas Chasidei Chabad.

HER PASSING

he Rebbetzin passed away on Wednesday, the 22nd of Shevat, 1988, after a brief illness. Her burial took place a few

hours afterwards at the Chabad cemetery in Queens, New York.

Rebbetzin Shterna Sarah

Shortly before her passing, Rebbetzin Chaya Mushka requested a glass of water. After reciting the blessing, "*...by Whose word all things come into being*," she returned her soul to her Maker.

In a farewell to a true queen, the funeral procession was fifteen thousand strong, led by an official police motorcade.

She was interred next to her grandmother, Rebbetzin Shterna Sarah, and near her father, Rabbi Yosef Yitzchak.

The Rebbe pointed out that Rabbi Yosef Yitzchak passed away in Shevat, as did his grandmother, Rebbetzin Rivka, his mother, Rebbetzin Shterna Sarah, and his daughter, Rebbetzin Chaya Mushka.

The Rebbe saying Kaddish for the Rebbetzin

HER LEGACY

The afternoon following the funeral, the Rebbe called in his secretary, Rabbi Yehuda Krinsky, and among other things instructed him to establish, as quickly as possible, a *tzedakah*-fund to be named for the Rebbetzin, of blessed memory.

Before the end of *Shiva*, "Keren Hachomesh" was established (an acronym of the first letters of the names Harabbonis Chaya Mushka Schneerson) at Lubavitch World Headquarters, which continually serves a variety of needy causes, primarily women's social and educational purposes.

קרן
החמ ש

During the following years, the Rebbe distributed significant sums from this fund to Chabad institutions and individuals all over the world.

Sunday, the 24th of Adar, 1988, was marked by the laying of the cornerstone for "Campus Chomesh," in memory of the Rebbetzin. Near the conclusion of the momentous event, the Rebbe himself suddenly arrived.

From the car window the Rebbe handed Rabbi Avraham Shemtov 470 dollars (numerically equivalent to "Chaya Mushka") saying: *I am on the way to the Ohel, and I shall visit her (resting place) as well. Tonight is her*

birthday, and this (sum) is my participation and her participation in this new edifice.

Today, Campus Chomesh is the largest Jewish girls' school in the world.

In the years following her passing, hundreds of Lubavitch institutions around the world have been established in honor of her memory, many *mikvahs* bear her name and numerous publications and periodicals were also dedicated to her memory.

On Monday, the 25th of Adar, 1988, the Rebbetzin's birthday, the Rebbe announced a special Birthday-Campaign in honor of the Rebbetzin. The campaign popularized birthday customs such as increasing one's Torah study, prayer, and the giving of charity. The campaign also encouraged everyone (even children) to hold a festive gathering together with family members or friends.

THE NAME
CHAYA MUSHKA

Chaya means life; Mushka, an aromatic spice.

On the significance of naming a child after the Rebbetzin, the Rebbe said:

". . .We can demonstrate that 'her children are alive,' by our taking a lesson from her conduct, and conducting ourselves in her spirit, in a manner of self-sacrifice.

"This is even more so when naming a child after her, and training the child to follow her example. After all, this is the most basic aspect of 'her children are alive, so too is she alive.'. . ."

The Rebbetzin had no children of her own, yet when a child visiting her at home asked her 'where are your children?' she answered that the Chasidim were her children. In return, today, thousands of baby girls have been given her name.

*H*er striking regal bearing, her gentle sense of humor, and her compassionate, considerate and sensitive manner, endeared her to all. She remains unforgettable by all who knew her.

פ״נ

הרבנית הצדקנית

מרת **חי׳ מושקא**

בת כ״ק אדמו״ר

אור עולם

נזר ישראל ותפארתו

צדקה ה׳ עשה

ומשפטיו עם ישראל

ורבים השיב מעון

מרנא ורבנא

יוסף יצחק

ובת הרבנית הצדקנית

מרת **נחמה דינה**

ע״ה ז״ל

נפטרה

ביום רביעי פ׳ משפטים

כ״ב שבט שנת ה׳תשמ״ח

ת׳ נ׳ צ׳ ב׳ ה׳

ולז״נ אחותה הרבנית הצדקנית

מרת **שיינא**

הי״ד

At the bottom of the Rebbetzin's headstone there is a memorial for her sister Sheina

The Rebbetzin's Shabbos candlesticks

Sources:
Lubavitch News Service • Hayom Yom • Igrot Kodesh (Rashab), Vol. 3 • Yemei Melech • Ashkavta D'rebbe • Agudas Chasidei Chabad Tenth Anniversary Journal Ateret Malchut • Days In Chabad • Sichat Adar 25, 5748 • Sichat Kislev 14, 5714 Sichat Shabbat Parshat Yitro, Shevat 22, 5749 • Kuntres Chof-Chet Sivan K'far Chabad Magazine, vol. 748 • The Heroic Struggle • All the Days of Her Life

Credits:
Editor: Shmuel M. Marcus • Photo Credits: S. Roumani, Agudas Chasidei Chabad Library • Maps: M. Lewis • Design: Spotlight Design Inc.